Lessons for Young Ladies In Waiting

By
Minister Anita Michelle Lewis

Lessons for Young Ladies in Waiting
Copyright © 2008 Anita Michelle Lewis
All Rights Reserved

ISBN: 978-1-59352-408-1
Published by:
Christian Services Network
1975 Janich Ranch Ct.
El Cajon, CA 92019

Toll Free: 1-866-484-6184
www.CSNbooks.com

No part of this publication may be reproduced, stored in a retrieval system, or transmitted in any way by any means – electronic, mechanical, photocopy, recording, or otherwise, without the prior permission of the copyright holder, except as provided by USA copyright law.

Unless otherwise stated all Scripture is taken from the King James Version of the Bible.

Printed in the United States of America.

Special Acknowledgements

First and foremost, I would like to thank God, who is truly the Lover of my Soul. He is my Lifesaver. I thank Him for choosing me, despite all of my past failures and present faults, to share His love and grace. I thank Him for my life and for the testimony that He has blessed me to share through this book.

Second, I would like to acknowledge my wonderful husband, David. Boo Bell, you are truly my best friend and one true love. Thank you for battling for and with me in the spirit. Thank you for loving me so completely. Thank you for being my king and my covering. From the beginning, you ministered to the wounded girl in me, treating me like a queen until I believed and felt like one.

I also want to thank all of the people who prayed for me as I was going through the difficult times in my life and who continue to pray for me. Thank you to my parents, Pastors Odell and Elaine Shaw, siblings, and grandmother for their continued love and support. Thank you to my Lynchburg family who looked out for me while I was in college and stood in the gap for me. Thanks to my special girlfriends (you know who you are) for loving me and accepting me as I am. To my spiritual parents, Pastor Steve and Pastor Wanda, thank you for inspiring me to dream big and helping me on my road to complete deliverance.

The Word that comes from out of your mouths each week is life to me. HGI Family, I love you!

Last, but not least, I want to acknowledge everyone who assisted me through the process of writing and publishing my book. Whether you prayed, encouraged, proofed, or advised, I thank you. If I didn't mention you by name, charge it to my head, not to my heart. To all the people at CSN, I could not have done this without you!

TABLE OF CONTENTS

Special Acknowledgements iii
My Story..vii
Introduction:... xiii
    What Is A Lady?

Lesson 1:..17
    Know Your God
Lesson 2...27
    Know Whose You Are
Lesson 3...35
    Know Who You Are
Lesson 4...43
    Be an Eagle, Not a Chicken
Lesson 5:... 57
    Run, Lady, Run!
Lesson 6...65
    Don't Believe the Hype
Lesson 7...75
    Keep It Real
Lesson 8...87
    It's A Love Thang
Lesson 9...99
    True Love Waits
Special Note...111

My Story

"No!" I yelled, tears streaming down my eyes. "Mommy, no!" I cried out in agony, as the words of the doctor sank into my heart from my head. Is what I am hearing true? Can this really be? "There should be a signal of a heart beat right there," he said, pointing at the screen. "He or she must have been gone for at least a week because the development is only at 9 weeks." I stared into the deep, blue eyes of the doctor. His eyes were clearly filled with a pity I neither wanted nor needed. What I wanted and so desperately needed was to wake up from this nightmare. I turned my head towards the screen, staring in wonder at my baby. I said a silent prayer. *God, please don't do this to me! I can't take it!* I willed my baby to fight. *Fight for mommy. Don't give up.* No response. I reached my hand out, touching the screen, thinking maybe if she felt me, felt my touch, she would see how much I needed her, how much I already loved her. *Come on, baby. Fight. Just breathe.* But, it was too late. The doctor, having finished his business, turned off the screen, and silently left the room, my mother following after him. Our connection was gone. She had lost the fight. I had lost my baby.

Years later, I still remember that experience. I can still see the blue eyes of the doctor, the furry figure of my baby on the screen, the stark whiteness of the walls in the examining room. I remember the feelings—of disappointment from my parents, disappointment in myself, hurt, anger, and isolation. Most importantly, I remember the breaking. It was an unmistakable break in my heart and my spirit. I could almost physically feel it and hear it. I had broken away from my God and, I felt at the time, He had broken away from me. After all, I had committed a great sin in having sex before marriage. Wasn't I supposed to be saved? Wasn't I supposed to love Him and obey His Word? My miscarriage was punishment for my hypocrisy, my penance for my sin of loving someone to the point that I was willing to sin, of not loving God enough. From that moment on, my whole perception of God and my walk changed. God was to be feared. He was quick to render justice, quick to get angry. I was not worthy of His love, His mercy.

I went off to college and spent the next four years trying to make up for what I had done. I made good grades. I was active on campus. I stayed out of trouble. I even got involved in a local church. I made everyone back home proud of me. The pregnancy was forgiven and forgotten. The miscarriage was seen as an unfortunate event. On the surface, I was doing fine. I was usually the happy one, the one that had it together, and the one that others came to for advice and support. Inside, however, I was not whole. Images of that day haunted me in my dreams and in my waking hours. Sometimes when I walked across campus or lay in my room at night, I would hear a baby crying. I thought about the procedure that they had to perform, the fact that what little existed of my baby was scraped and ripped from me. I thought about the God who had let me down, and had let my baby die, but I also thought about the God who I had learned about from childhood and still heard about—the God who was loving and forgiving. I could not reconcile the two pictures in my head and it was driving me crazy.

In the midst of all of this, I was still having sex. In fact, in addition to the young man who was the father of my baby, I had two more sexual partners in college. I justified it by telling myself that I was in monogamous, committed relationships, that I was not promiscuous. The truth is that I was trying to fill the emptiness inside by having sex. I needed to feel wanted. The sad reality is that I felt even more empty and dirty after having sex. I just could not get out of the cycle I had created for myself. By senior year, I had gotten to the point where I did not care to justify any of my actions. I just wanted to do what I wanted to do. I was so tired of the façade, tired of pleasing everyone, and tired of being so good. I felt so fake, so empty inside. I did not know who I was or who I wanted to be. I still went through the motions. No one would have ever known that I cried myself to sleep at night or cried in the mornings because I did not want to get out of bed. No one knew that I had begun to wish for death.

My lowest point came when I thought I was pregnant again. Instead of being happy or accepting of this fact, I went to a clinic to get an abortion. As I lay on the table, I wondered how I had gotten to this point, that I was willing to do something that I did not believe in just to keep up my façade and not have my life interrupted. It turned out that I was not pregnant, but just the fact that I was willing to get an abortion tore at my very core.

People say that God knows what you need even before you ask, and that He shows up just in time. Well, I never knew the meaning of that statement until one morning when my phone rang. It was a woman from my local church who had become my spiritual mother, someone my mother trusted to look after me. She said that she needed to see me right away. We met at the church, where she informed me that my mother had called her and asked her to intervene. My mother sensed that something was going on with me, but was too far away. She wanted someone close to me to pray with and for me. At first, my spiritual mother was going to wait until the weekend, but during her prayer time God prompted her to call me right away. She shared with me that He told her that the devil was trying to kill me. As I sat across the table

My Story

from her, a denial began to form on my lips. After almost four years of wearing a mask, never really letting anyone see all of me, was I ready to tell all? In that moment, something stirred on the inside of me. A voice said, *"Your life depends on it."* For the second time in my life, I felt another breaking. This time, it was a wall, and it felt so good.

For the next two years, I spent time getting to know myself, and reestablishing my relationship with God. I learned so much during that time. Now I sit many years after my miscarriage, ready to share these valuable lessons. I by no means have arrived, nor am I suggesting that I know it all. I feel compelled, however, to tell my story and share these lessons for several reasons. First, it is my desire to spare any young lady of the hurt and shame that comes from having sex before marriage. Hopefully, my experience will convince at least one young lady to wait until she is married. I encourage you to purchase a journal prior to reading my book. Write down your thoughts and questions as you read. At the end of each chapter, I included practical tools that I think are useful for you to implement. Write about how you can implement these tools. In other words, don't just read for the sake of reading. Allow the words to move you towards action. Second, I feel that it is important for parents and religious youth leaders to understand what happens to a young lady— mentally, emotionally, and spiritually—when she engages in sex before marriage. They need to be real and open in their discussions about sex. It is not enough to say don't have sex. It is not even enough to say it is a sin. Real life examples work. More importantly, tools for how to wait, how to say no, how to handle what they are feeling is what's needed to help them abstain. Prayerfully, the tools that I discuss in the book will help. Finally, this book is an act of service to God. I am so appreciative of the second chance that He has given me. My life could have ended in death by my own hand, but God held back the enemy and sent me help. Now, it is my duty to share what He has shown me and has given me with others so that they can become ladies in waiting.

Introduction:

What is a Lady?

"Just because you're a female does not mean that you are a lady." This is something that I have said to many of my female students throughout my six years of teaching and two years of counseling. All of them wanted to declare themselves as ladies, even women, but very few of them realized what it truly takes to be a lady. Webster Dictionary has several definitions for the word "lady", but one sticks out to me the most—*a woman of rank and distinction.* Now you might ask, "Well, how can that apply to me when I have neither?" Here is the problem of many young females. They have no idea that they not only have rank and distinction; they also have dominion. They have had it from the beginning.

The first chapter of Genesis tells the story of creation. The most important creation was mankind. Verses 26-30 tell us that God made male and female in His image. Not only this, but it gives very specific directives for our lives, one of which is "*...and let them have **dominion**...*" From the very beginning, God separated us from every other living thing on earth. He distinguished us and set us apart for His purposes. Another directive given is to "***subdue** the earth*". Subdue means to conquer, to bring into subjection, and to prevail over. Thus, not only did He set us apart, but he also set us *over* the things of this earth.

What does all of this mean? It means that **those of us who belong to God** (notice the bold print) have both distinction and rank. Our distinction lies in the fact that God has separated us and esteemed us higher than any of His other creations. He predestined from the very beginning that we would be at the center of creation and the focus of His love. (See Ephesians 1:3-6). Our rank lies in the fact that we belong to a class of people who are excellent because we serve an excellent, all powerful, and almighty God who can do anything but fail. As a result, whenever we are in trouble, whenever we need help, whenever we need answers or directions for our lives, we can "pull rank" and call on our God. We can also pull down and subdue anything that threatens our position in the earth.

My fall resulted from my not realizing my distinction and rank as a child of God. I did not know what I was created for and how much power I had over the forces that were pulling me from my rightful place. Every time I had sex, I was pulled further and further away from my God and,

Introduction

ultimately, my position and all of the privileges that came with it. See, being a child of God means more than just having dominion over the earth. It also means experiencing all that is good—peace, love, and joy. I cheated myself for so long. Now, I am glad to say that I am experiencing all that is good as I fully embrace my role as a woman of God. I would not be able to do this had I not been open to the lessons God had for me to learn from that difficult period in my life. I must say that there were times when I cried from shame and disgust as I slowly opened myself up to hear from God and, as a result, to the ugly truths about myself. Once I faced myself and came clean with my God, I became whole.

Today, I continue to be a lady in waiting. I hope that after reading my lessons, you will join me and take your rightful place in God's kingdom.

Lessons for Young Ladies in Waiting

Lesson 1:

"Know Your God"

Scripture Reference: Isaiah 45:5-6

Have you ever been accused of something that you did not do? Or has someone ever come to you and told you that someone close to you said or did something? In either case you, or that someone close to you, can be vindicated on the basis of one thing—what people know to be true of your character. Even in the court of law, when someone is accused of something, the defense calls upon character witnesses. These witnesses are people who can testify about what type of individual that person is. They usually can attest to the individual's kindness, respectfulness, honesty, and integrity. These witnesses are called to testify because they truly know the individual based on their own personal experiences with that individual over a period of time. It is easy to trust, respect, and love someone that you know, someone whose good character you have seen in action. But, this trust, love, and respect are developed over time and after experiences with the individual. This is what it takes to truly get to know someone, including God.

Many of us today would say that we know God. If anyone asked me when I was a teenager if I knew God, I would have said yes. I had accepted Jesus as my Savior. I went to church faithfully every Sunday and Wednesday. I read my bible periodically and tried to pray every morning or night. Many of you do the same. Does this mean that you know God? No. Knowing God is not about following the practices of your church. It is not about an occasional reading of your bible or praying at night before you go to bed because it is the right thing to do. Knowing God is a matter of your heart and your will. It is about forging a bond, a real relationship with the One who created you. In some ways, getting to know God is very similar to getting to know any individual on earth.

Getting to Know Him

How do you get to know someone? You talk to them. You express interest in knowing their likes and dislikes, their habits, and their strengths and weaknesses. Over time, as trust and respect are built, you may even trade intimate secrets with

Lesson 1: Know Your God

them. You share in their life experiences. You spend quality time with them.

You may think that it cannot possibly be this simple to get to know God. You may be thinking that getting to know the Creator, the Almighty, Wonderful, and All-Powerful God must involve some mysterious, deep process, right? Wrong! In fact, it is probably easier to get to know God than people once you are willing to put in the time and energy. Getting to know people can be more complicated for two reasons. First, people are constantly changing on you. They can be one way on any given day and completely different on another. Second, people are moved by what is going on around them. Their emotions, actions, and attitudes are often predetermined by what they see, hear, and experience. Fortunately, God does not have these attributes.

The Bible tells us that God never changes. In fact, He is *"the same yesterday, today, and forevermore."* (Hebrews 13:8) It goes on to say that all that He does and says is forever. (Numbers 23:19; Ecclesiastes 3:14; Isaiah 40:8) This means that you can trust Him. God does not lie. He does not go back on His promises. He means what He says. God also is not moved by what is going on in the earth or even in our personal lives. Now, let me explain what I mean by "not moved". I mean that He is not flustered or puzzled or incapacitated. When things go on in our lives or the world around us, God knows what to do and how to do it. Unlike people, He does not change his attitude or feelings towards us. This is even the case when we mess up and make a mistake or when everything seems to be going wrong. His love is never failing and never ending. His strength is unconquerable; His wisdom incomparable.

Because God is never changing and is not moved by what goes on, He is easy to know. It starts with making up in your mind that you want to get to know God. Then, you set your heart and will to follow through with this desire. Why? Often times, it will be an act of your will because your flesh may not feel like doing what it takes—time and effort. If we look back at the steps I listed above to get to know someone, they are applicable to your developing a relationship with God. First, you should talk to Him every day. Think of your closest friend. If you did not talk to him/her every day, you would miss out on sharing your thoughts and feelings with someone you care about and vice-versa. You also might miss out on something important that happened. Well, if you miss talking to God every day, you will not have the opportunity to share your thoughts, worries, feelings, and plans for the day with the One who created you. Not only that, you will miss out on hearing from God the necessary direction and guidance for the day. Remember, God is all seeing and all knowing. Thus, there may be something that He foresees that He wants to protect you from, prepare you for, or help you to avoid altogether. Second, you should read His Word every day. This is how God communicates His likes and dislikes, His ways, and His will for our lives. God also reveals His promises. How can we develop any trust if we do not have any Word to stand on and try in times of difficulty and temptation? Without trust, any relationship is shaky.

The Benefits of Knowing Him

One of the things that I love about being in a true relationship with God is that I reap so many benefits. It's not like some friendships or relationships that I have been in where I seem to be doing all of the giving and not receiving anything in return. The closer I get to God and the more I come to know Him, the more blessings that come my way.

Benefit One: To know Him is to experience Him. As you get to know God, you will open yourself up to experience who He truly is.

Benefit Two: To experience Him is to love and trust Him. The more experiences you have with God, the more you witness His goodness, mercy, and power on your behalf, the more you will begin to love Him and trust Him. The trust issue is a serious one because it is the devil's desire to form a rift between you and God. One way that He does this is to get you not to trust

God. When you do not trust God, your faith is weak and you are subject to fall for anything (and anyone). You are moved by what you see because you do not trust the One who knows all. When things go wrong, your lack of trust may cause you to blame God and become angry, which was what happened in my situation.

Benefit Three: To love Him is to obey Him. When you love God the way we are commanded to love God—with all of our heart, soul, and strength—you will be compelled to obey Him. It will be hard to disobey because your heart is turned towards Him, and you do not want to disappoint the One you love.

Benefit Four: To obey Him is to walk into bountiful blessings. The twenty-eighth chapter of Deuteronomy tells us of all the blessings we are entitled to when we obey God. Some see obeying God as something that is a burden. They do not understand that God asks for obedience both as a sign of our love for Him and His love for us. God is not trying to control us or take something from us. He is trying to get things to us. Think about it, so many of God's commands are linked to blessings and promises. For example, in Deuteronomy 8, God promised the Israelites if they loved Him with all of their heart, soul, and might, that He would *"give them great and goodly cities, which thou buildest not,*

Lesson 1: Know Your God

and houses full of good things, which thou fillest not…". In today's terms, this simply means that when you and I love God with our whole being, then we will walk in prosperity. He will bless us with material and spiritual blessings that we do not even have to work to obtain. In a few chapters over, chapter 11, God promises that their days will be multiplied and every place where they tread their feet will be theirs. This means that loving God completely yields long life. It also means that wherever you go, you can walk in authority. No, you will not "own" everything. Let me put it this way. Are you believing God to be accepted into a certain college or for a position on a team, an office in Student Council, or a role in the school play? Could some of you be trusting God for a job? Well, whatever you desire and wherever you place your feet and declare is yours can be yours!

Practical Ways to Get to Know Him

1. Establish a regular "quiet time". This is a consistent, daily, uninterrupted time that you spend with God. Use this time to pray and to read your Word. You may want to purchase some devotionals geared towards people your age to assist you in your study of the Word. Try to choose devotionals that will interest you and cover areas you may be struggling in or have questions about. Your "quiet time" should be

unique to who you are. God does not expect you to mimic what your parents or other people do. He wants you to come to Him in a way that is comfortable for you, in a way that makes it easy for you to relate to Him. So, if you need to have soft worship music playing, do that. If you need to incorporate some praise music to get you going, do that. Whatever it is, do not neglect that time. It may seem awkward or even boring at first, but the more you do it, the more your desire for Him will increase.

2. Attend church regularly. Some people take their church attendance lightly, but the Bible actually instructs us not to *"forsake the assembly of ourselves"* (Hebrews 10: 25). Find a church that has strong teaching and an active youth ministry. If you are in a situation where your parents do not attend church regularly or at all, find a friend who is willing to take you along. Some churches also have van services that will pick you up. Attending church regularly is important because it gives you two things—a spiritual father and/or mother who can teach, pray for and advise you, as well as a spiritual family who can help and encourage you to live for Him.

3. Be active in your church. It is never too early to get involved in church. Serving God is a way to get closer to Him. Most churches today have a youth ministry. Attend their fellowships and special services. Seek out other

Lesson 1: Know Your God

opportunities to serve, such as the dance or step team, the choir, the drama ministry, and/or the sound ministry.

4. Realize that God wants to know you. From the beginning, God desired to be in a close relationship with mankind. His whole reason for sending His son was so that we could regain that relationship that began with Him and Adam in Eden. Think about it. The most powerful, wise, and almighty God gave up His only son so that we could know Him and He could lavish His love on us!

5. Finally, be open. God is all around us. Be attentive and watchful for the teachable moments. Do not wait for your "quiet time" to talk to God or acknowledge His goodness. He is always there, and it is okay to "steal" a few moments to spend time with Him. He is always available and waiting with open arms.

Lessons for Young Ladies in Waiting

Lesson 2:

Know Whose You Are

Scripture Reference: Isaiah 43: 1; I Corinthians 6: 19-20

"You not my mother. You don't own me! You can't tell me what to do!" I cannot tell you how many times I have heard students say this to their teachers. As a counselor, I have had to intervene between teachers and their students, some who think that they are untouchable and above being corrected. There are some who walk around with an air of entitlement at home and at school, thinking that they are free to do whatever they want. They do not believe that they have to answer to someone for their actions. This is the case even in the world at large. Some people lavish in their freedom to choose how they want to live and conduct themselves in their homes, on their jobs, and in public. With this freedom comes a sense of personal responsibility that some fail to realize and assume. For this reason, some people live lives that are void of any real moral standards for themselves. Others appear to have standards, only to be exposed to have "secret lives" that shock those around them.

The church is not innocent of this trend. Even among God's people, there are people who lack character and live their lives thinking that they do not have to assume any personal responsibility or consequences for their actions. Others lead "secret lives", doing things behind closed doors that they know go against God's will for their lives. However, unlike the world, it is very clear to those of us who are saved that we have to answer to someone. In fact, we have to answer to the One.

You Are Not Your Own

One of the greatest gifts that God gave to man was freewill. He even allows us to choose Him. What we have to realize is that, though we do have freewill, once we choose to accept salvation, we belong to Him. This does not take away our freedom to choose, but it does, or at least should, determine/govern our choices as we go through our lives. First Corinthians 6:19-20 makes it very clear for us. *"What? Know ye not that your body is the temple of the Holy Ghost, which is in you, which ye have of God, and ye are not your own? For ye are bought with a price: therefore glorify God in your body, and in your spirit, which are God's."* This

Lesson 2: Know Whose You Are

scripture lets us know several things. First, our bodies are temples. As temples, our bodies are supposed to be worthy of the One who dwells in them. Thus, they must be pure and holy. Second, God has bought us with a price. This wording may upset some, but it is the truth. In fact, He has paid the highest price anyone can pay—the price of His son's life. Third, this scripture guides us in our choices. It lets us know that whatever we choose to do, wherever we choose to go, and whatever we choose to say, should glorify God.

Danger Zone

The Israelites were God's chosen people. He delivered them out of slavery and promised to lead them to a wonderful land where they would not have to lack for anything. All He asked of them was that they love, obey, and fear Him. God also continued to admonish them not to forget who He was. Unfortunately, the Israelites did not heed God's request. Time and time again, they strayed away, seeking to do their own thing. It got to be so bad, that the first generation that was led out of Egypt never got to live to see the Promised Land because of their disobedience. They wandered around aimlessly in the wilderness. Despite the punishment received by their ancestors, generations that followed still struggled with disobedience. They, too, wanted to do their own thing. As a result, they went in and out of years of captivity and other hard times, such as famine, disease, and extreme poverty.

Today, God makes the same request of His people. God is saying, *"Love me as I have loved you—totally and unselfishly. Do not forget who I am. I am the true and living God. Beside me, there is no other. I am all-powerful and mighty. I am your deliverer. I am your creator. You belong to me! Serve me, respect me, honor me, and I will give you all that you desire. I will give you the world!"* Yes, God wants to give us the world, but we want to do things our way. We forget the One who has created us, the One who has chosen us. We forget it is He who gives us life, health, and strength. It is He who has given us the talents, skills, and abilities that we have. It is all about Him!

There is a danger in forgetting that you belong to the most-high God. God reminds us in His Word that he is a jealous God. In other words, He cannot tolerate anyone or anything being put above or before Him. He desires to have His rightful place in our lives and hearts. In Isaiah 43: 21, He reminds us that we were formed for Him, to proclaim His praise. We were not created to live for ourselves, to fulfill our own wills. Everything we do should show forth praise to our Creator. When we forget whom we belong to and the place that He should have in our lives, we risk missing out on the promises of God just like the Israelites. We experience a spiritual famine.

Lesson 2: Know Whose You Are

I thought that having sex was going to give me fulfillment. In the end, I felt more emptiness, loss, and shame. I now strongly believe that having sex before marriage is the ultimate misuse and mistreatment of your body. It also is a rejection of God as your great Creator and King. Every time I had sex, I was basically saying that I belonged to myself, and that I could do whatever I wanted to and with my body, even lend it to the hands of young men who did not love or cherish me the way God intended. I forgot that I was made for His good pleasure. I sought to please others, namely men, with my body. I was in a dangerous place because I was spitting in the face of God. I shiver at the thought of what could have been—more pregnancies, an actual abortion, STD's, HIV, or even death. I thank God that I remembered Him and who He is in time.

But, so many people do not. They live their lives as if it's their own. We all have heard that saying, "You only have one life to live." Some people take this as a license to live life without any inhibitions, to do what feels right or what they think is right. They may even argue that following God while they are young keeps them from living complete, fun-filled lives. They would rather wait until they are older to serve God. The Bible tells us in Proverbs 14:12, however, that *"There is a way which seemeth right unto a man, but the end thereof are the ways of death."* People who live their lives in a way that is "right for them" will ultimately find themselves on destructive paths. How can you possibly live a fulfilled life, if you do not follow the One who created you? After all, the Creator knows what you need. He knows what paths you should take, and which you should avoid. He knows your dreams and desires. If you do not acknowledge Him and remember Him in your living, you will experience the ways of death—emptiness, loss, and unfulfillment.

Solomon, a king who fell prey to his own fleshly desires, encourages young people in Ecclesiastes 12:1 to remember God while they are young. He did not want them to live as he lived, giving in to his flesh and living to regret it later in life. Yes, you only have one life to live. Live it remembering who God is. Live a life that you will not look back on with so many regrets.

Practical Ways To Remember Whose You Are

1. Begin each morning with acknowledging God as both your Creator and your Source. Thank Him for life and for allowing you to see another day.

2. Go throughout your day acknowledging God. Thank Him for giving you the strength to make it through a difficult test or talk to a difficult teacher. Thank Him for blessing you

Lesson 2: Know Whose You Are

with a job and helping you deal with an unfair boss or a moody customer. Thank Him for your ability to see, hear, walk, smell, and taste. Thank Him for everything!

3. Dedicate every part of yourself to Him—mind, body, will, and emotions. Do not be afraid to surrender. In surrender there is freedom.

4. As you go throughout the day, ask yourself if God would be pleased with what you have selected to wear, how you are carrying yourself, what you are saying, and what you are thinking. Remember, you were created for His good pleasure. Would God be please with you? If not, make the necessary adjustments.

Lessons for Young Ladies in Waiting

Lesson 3:

Know Who You Are

Scripture Reference: 1 Peter 2: 9

I struggled with low self-esteem for the longest time. From middle school well into my early twenties, I felt that I was not pretty enough, "thick" enough, or dressed good enough. There was even a time when I did not feel that I was "black" enough. As a result, I failed to see and appreciate the many good qualities that I did have. I failed to get to know myself for who I truly was because I was caught up in what other people thought or said about who I was. More importantly, I failed to love myself. This led to me making the poor choices that I did as it related to relationships and several other areas in my life.

Not knowing who you are and not loving yourself can put you in a very vulnerable place. You become more susceptible and sensitive to the scrutiny and criticism of others. You also tend to change like the weather, meaning that you switch up depending on whom you are around. You wear several faces and try on various personas. Soon, you lose yourself and find that you are further away from knowing who you are or being who God called you to be.

Dear One, I know what it is to search for identity. It is the search of every adolescent. I know what it is to struggle between who you want to be, who your parents want you to be, and who your friends want you to be. I wore masks for a long time. I faked it for a long time, revealing only parts of the real me. Then I realized that I could not fully know or love myself until I knew who I was called to be in Him. My identity was and is in Him. It is in Him that your identity lays as well. All you have to do is seek Him and He will show you who you are.

What God Says About You

I often like to refer to the Bible as a love letter from God. It is filled with scriptures from God to us revealing how He sees us. Whenever I get down or feel those old feelings of worthlessness rising up, I like to read certain scriptures to remind me of how much God loves me and how precious and worthy I am in His eyes. After reading them, I always close my Bible in awe of who God created me to be and how He sees me. It gives me a sense of peace, joy,

Lesson 3: Know Who You Are

and yes, relief to know that God sees me in such a marvelous way. I hope they do the same for you as well. Enjoy.

I Peter 2:9 *"But ye are a <u>chosen</u> generation, a <u>royal</u> priesthood, a holy nation, a peculiar people."* I have underlined two words: "chosen" and "royal". The first lets me know that I have been selected by God, that He wanted me to be His; while the second word tells me that I am royalty. As royalty, I have distinction, power, and authority. Being royalty also grants me certain rights. I have a right to good health, peace of mind, joy, wealth, and the good life. I also have the right to be treated as the queen God says that I am. I should be treated with respect and honor. With that right comes a responsibility as well. I must carry myself like a queen at all times so that I can obtain all of the rights and privileges of God's Kingdom. God is looking for His queens. Will you be among them?

Psalm 139:14
"I will praise thee for I am fearfully and wonderfully made: marvelous are thy works; and that my soul knoweth well."

I love this scripture because it tells me that God makes no mistakes or, as some would say, "God don't make no junk!" The word "fearfully" in this text means with reverence. I was made to be respected and admired. God also considers me to be a wonderful, marvelous creation. The most important part of the scripture is not in the description, but in the psalmist's confident statement. His *"soul knoweth well"*. He can praise God because His soul (mind, will, and emotions) rests in the knowledge of who he is in God. When you know with all of your being that you are wonderful, marvelous, and to be respected, you can't help but to love yourself and the One who created you.

> Jeremiah 29:11
> *For I know the thoughts that I think toward you, saith the Lord, thoughts of peace, and not of evil, to give you an expected end.*

I like to refer to this as one of my "life scriptures". For one, I quote this scripture everyday. It reminds me that I can live my day in peace and joy because God is thinking of me and working on my behalf. Second, this scripture saved my life. When I realized that God not only loved me, but also had me on His mind, it gave me hope. In fact, **He was not wishing evil upon me. He wanted good things for me. He also had an end for me. That meant I had a future! I could not die. I had to live to see what God had in store just for me! God has a future for you**, too. He wants to see you live your days in peace and joy. Your expected end can be nothing but successful with God as the mastermind.

Lesson 3: Know Who You Are

Hebrews 13:5 *"I will never leave thee, nor forsake thee."* What a great promise, because it means that you and I are never alone. **Do not let the devil tell you that you need a man to fight off loneliness**. I did lots of stupid things because I did not want to be alone. Now I know that God is always with me. He is always with you. Does that mean you will not want companionship, even that of the opposite sex? No, but if you seek God, He will give you the strength to fight off the temptation of seeking comfort from the opposite sex. He will also surround you with holy "distractions" if you allow Him to—work, church, Christian friends, hobbies, activities, etc. Do not forget that God is the greatest fulfillment. He wants to be your closest friend. Can you believe it? The great God promises to stick by you through everything. No matter who leaves you or gives up on you, you can always count on God being there. No matter how many times you make a mistake, you can always count on God being there. You are that important to Him and He loves you so much, that **He cannot** bring **Himself to leave you**.

Practical Ways to Know Who You Are

Knowing who you are is an ongoing process as you grow and evolve throughout the stages of your life. Is it possible to know who you are as an adolescent female? Yes and no. No, because you still have much development to do emotionally and mentally. You can know lots of things about your personality. You can also know your strengths, weaknesses, faults, and pet peeves. You do have some dreams and a vision of what you would like your life to be. Some of these things will change, however, as you grow and have more experiences. Even when you become an adult, you still will have times when you have to get "reacquainted" with yourself.

Now, knowing who you are in Him is a much different story. Why? Because He shows you in His word. It is just a matter of reading it, grasping it, believing it, and living it. Here's how:

1. Read self-affirming scriptures daily. You can start with the few that I have given you and add to them. Commit them to memory so that you can remind yourself of how God sees you whenever you are feeling down.

2. Write self-affirming words on index cards and display them. I have written scriptures, positive sayings, and even inspirational points from sermons on index cards and taped them around the house. You can do this in your room, locker, notebooks, etc. This way, these words are always before you. If they are always before you, it is easier to make them a reality.

Lesson 3: Know Who You Are

3. Surround yourself with positive people who encourage and support you. There is nothing worse than having a friend or group of friends who are always negative and/or cannot celebrate anyone but themselves. You want to hang around people who see the positive in you, can be honest about that which you need to work on, and encourage you in your efforts to be better. You also need people who can celebrate you and your accomplishments, whether it's a new hairdo, passing a test, getting a job, getting into college, etc.

4. "Talk good" to yourself. Now, some may think this is crazy, but sometimes, I have to look myself in the mirror and "talk good" to myself. Yes, I actually compliment myself and go through my accomplishments. I remind myself of my strengths and my talents. This is not being conceited. This is a way of putting yourself, and the devil, on notice. You are not going to struggle with low self-esteem; you are not going to get down on yourself; and you are not going to "talk down" to yourself! You are a child of the king, and He does not make junk!

Lessons for Young Ladies in Waiting

Lesson 4:

Be An Eagle, Not A Chicken

Scripture Reference: Romans 12: 2

    There is a short tale by Michael Wynn called *The Eagles Who Thought They Were Chickens*. The story is about baby eagles that were brought over to America in a slave ship. The eagles are taken to a plantation chicken yard where they are kept ignorant of their heritage and ridiculed by the chickens and the rooster overseer for being different. The rooster overseer makes their lives even more miserable by subjecting them to abuse and hard labor. As a result, these baby eagles lose their sense of identity. They are made to feel ugly and inferior, lacking any confidence in themselves as eagles and are unable to fly. They begin to live as the chickens. One day, the Great Eagle, an older, wiser eagle who survived the Middle Passage from Africa, flies to the plantation where the baby eagles are being held. Aware of his rich heritage, he informs the baby eagles of who they are. "We are not chickens. We come from a land rich in history and cultural heritage. We are not born to walk like chickens, but to soar through the clouds. We belong to a great and proud people." After listening to the Great Eagle, the baby eagles develop the positive self-image and confidence that they need to fly away, following the Great Eagle into their great destiny.

I find this to be such a fitting story for this book. See, these baby eagles not only suffered from a negative self-image, which I have touched on, they also suffered from being ignorant of their rich heritage and from conforming to the world around them. They allowed the world around them to dictate to them how they should live and how far they could go in life. If it had not been for the Great Eagle, these baby eagles would have been left in ignorance and conformity, never rising above their current situation.

These baby eagles represent all of you out there who have failed to realize your rich heritage. You are allowing yourselves to be molded and defined by the "chickens" of the world—the media, your current situation/status in life, your peers, and even your enemies. As if this is not enough, you even let the big rooster himself, the devil, run havoc in your emotions, your mind, and your life. But, I have good news for you. The Great Eagle, Jesus Christ, has come to free you from the confines of this world. He wants you to take your rightful place in the lineage of Christian royalty.

Lesson 4: Be an Eagle, Not a Chicken

Ignorance Is Not Bliss

One of my favorite subjects in school was American History. I loved hearing about times past—how people lived, dressed, acted, and thought. I enjoyed hearing about how things came to be and how things came to an end. When I got to college, I had the opportunity to take more classes in African and African American History. I read fiction and nonfiction about the struggles and accomplishments of my own ancestors. I felt for the first time a real connection with and pride in the past. I still enjoy reading historical fiction, set in different times and places that give a perspective on what it could have been like for African Americans back then. I also enjoy reading books that give actual accounts on historical events from people who were living at that time.

Many people, young and old, do not have the same appreciation for history. Some feel that it is boring. Others feel looking to the past is useless. They say, "The past is the past. It's dead." They feel that the present is most important. What they do now will propel them into their future. These people fail to realize the true value of history. History is not just an endless list of dates, people, and events. It is also about the beliefs, attitudes, and lifestyles of the past. It reveals the spirit of the people and the time in which they lived. History also serves to warn, inspire, and give direction. There is an old saying that goes, "If you don't know where you come from, you don't know where you are going." History gives us a sense of purpose, propelling us in the present towards the future. If acknowledged and understood, history can prevent us from making mistakes and/or give us the courage to move ahead.

Everyone has a history. We each have our individual histories, our own personal stories that are being developed with each passing day. We all have a family history, shared with people in the same bloodline. Lastly, we all share a common history with people of the same race and/or ethnicity. As Christians, we too, share a great history.

We come from a long line of men and women, dated back to the Bible, who have made great strides and accomplished wonderful things for, and with the help of, Jesus Christ.

Now, I know you may be asking yourself, "What do these people have to do with me?" You may feel that you have no use for old Bible stories about people who have been dead for centuries. Nor do you have any use for present day Christian leaders who sometimes seem so far removed from your own personal life. They cannot possibly understand what it is like to be young in today's time. They cannot possibly have anything to offer you, right? Well, think again.

Lesson 4: Be an Eagle, Not a Chicken

Looking at the Christian "heroes" from the Bible not only gives us examples and lessons on how to live right. It can also give today's Christians of all ages a clearer perspective of who we are in God and what we are entitled to because we belong to Him. See, when you become a Christian, you become a part of a lineage of greatness. You are no longer a part of the world's system and its way of living and thinking. Therefore, it does not matter what the world says is your status, your circumstance, or your limitations because you are now a part of God's Kingdom! Not convinced? Let me prove it to you.

Let's take a look at Abraham. Abraham was given a promise by God that He would do the following: make him into a great nation, bless him, make his name great, and cause him to be a blessing. He said that all people would be blessed through Abraham's seed/lineage. (See Genesis 12) Over in Genesis chapter 15, God also promises Abraham that He would be his shield, his reward, and his ever-increasing supply. If you examine Abraham's life, you will see that God blessed him with abundance in cattle, sheep, land, and workmen. In addition, God gave Abraham a child when he was 100 years old, which began a long line of one generation after another all the way to Jesus Christ. He outlived his wife, remarried, and went on to have six more children! When Abraham died, the Bible says that he lived 175 years. There is no record of sickness or disease in Abraham's life.

There is also no record of lack or defeat. He lived a life of blessing and prosperity, which was inherited by his son, Isaac, and is now transferred to every believer.

In Galatians 3: 29, we are told that, *"If you belong to Christ, then you are Abraham's seed, and heirs according to the promise."* Wow! This means that because we are saved and belong to Christ, we are entitled to the very same things that Abraham was promised. We can be blessed, our names can be great, we can be able to bless others, and we can live in prosperity. We just have to know where we come from, take our place in the lineage of Jesus Christ, and lay hold to what is rightfully ours! Many of us fail to do this. We allow the devil to trip us up, making us believe that those promises are only for "back in the day". He leads us to believe that we have to do things another way, the world's way, instead of relying on God's promises.

It is the devil's job to steal, kill, and destroy. He is a deceiver and a liar. He knows what God has for you, but wants to see you miss out. So, the devil leads some young people just like you down fast lanes and destructive paths that deceptively seem like the quick and easy ways to obtain wealth and happiness. This is how we get teenage drug dealers and handlers, teenage prostitutes, young, petty thieves, and bullies. You may say to yourself that you would never do such things. They are too bad. How about having sex to fulfill your physical and

Lesson 4: Be an Eagle, Not a Chicken

emotional needs? Or taking a quick hit here and there just to fit in? What about cheating on a test to make a good grade so that you can do well in a class or copying someone else's homework when you should have studied and did the work for yourself? Or how about telling a little "white lie" so that you do not get in trouble; or sneaking out of the house to go somewhere you know you are not supposed to go? You do certain things in an attempt to obtain some sense of happiness, fulfillment, and belonging—what you see as the good life.

There are other young people who the devil attacks in the mind. He tells them that they cannot possibly have a good life because of the things that they have done or the type of family that they come from. He gets them to focus on their circumstances and their supposed limitations. The devil feeds them lies, telling them that they are not good looking enough, smart enough, or popular enough. He makes them believe that God's promises do not apply to them. These people do not necessarily do anything to obtain a good life. Instead, they may be stagnant, immobile. Or, they may be indifferent. The devil may have beaten them down to the point where they are afraid to want anything more for themselves, or they have gotten to the point where they just do not care.

Whatever group you are in, your life will be a tragic one because of your ignorance to the truth and to God's promises. You will never fully reach your potential or achieve your dreams. In the end, the devil will eventually cheat you out of what God has for you and you will forfeit your inheritance. But, I encourage you, Dear One, to wake up. Do not be ignorant of the devil's scheme to cheat you. Do not be ignorant of your rich heritage. God's promises have not changed. He is the same yesterday, today, and forever. He will do what He said! Don't look for it anywhere else. Don't look for it from the world or from another human being. It is in Him. You are entitled. The baby eagles almost forfeited their inheritance, but listened to and applied the words of the Great Eagle. Listen to and believe the words of Christ, "***I have come that you might have life, and have it more abundantly.***"(John 10:10) Now live!

Come Out From Among Them

One of the most powerful elements from Abraham's story is what God commands Abraham to do before he obtains the promise. In Genesis 12:1, God says,

> *Leave your country, your people and your father's household and go to the land I will show you.*

Before God began to establish His promises in Abraham's life, Abraham had to leave his family and his friends. He had to leave behind his old way

Lesson 4: Be an Eagle, Not a Chicken

of life, everything that was familiar and comfortable to him had to be released. Why? For one, Abraham came from a people who were pagans. They did not believe in the true God. If Abraham had stayed, he might not have lived for God or followed after His ways. God was not in that place; therefore, His blessings could not be either. Secondly, God must have known that even if Abraham had stayed and tried to live for Him, he might have failed. The pressure to conform and fit in would have been too great. He would not have infected them with God; instead, they would have infected him with unrighteousness and unbelief.

This is what happened with the baby eagles. They were overpowered by the chickens and the rooster and forced to fit in. They had greatness on the inside of them that was being killed slowly day-by-day. Notice that when the Great Eagle came, he did not instruct them and then leave them where they were. He knew that they could not thrive in that environment. After all, that environment was not suitable for their design and purpose. They did not belong cackling on the ground, but flying high in the skies.

The Great Eagle gave them instruction, and then commanded them to leave so that they could take their rightful place.

See, grabbing hold to and obtaining the promises of God takes more than a mere belief. It takes action. You not only have to believe that you are an heir to a great inheritance; you also have to take your proper place. It will require you to reposition yourself. At your age, this can be hard. You have the desire to have friends and to fit in. You strive to be an individual, while at the same time you need to feel like you belong to something. But, it is important that you align yourself with the right people. It is important that you watch who you hang with and where you go. All people and all environments are not suitable for your design and your purpose. I am telling you straight from my heart—if I had been more cautious about whom I hung around, who I let get close to me, and where I went, I would not have ended up pregnant at 17. Please hear me. I have been there. I was not popular, but I was well liked and people knew me. I know what it is to be pressured to do things that you do not want to do. I know what it is to want a guy to like you so much that you allow him to do things to your body that you are not comfortable with, to go places with him that you should not go. I know what it is to take a hit or drink because everyone is watching. As a result, I wasted years. I spent almost 6 of my teen and young adult years conforming and not fully walking in my potential as a Christian or as a young woman. I spent another four years living in regret and healing from what I had done to myself! I could have been living the good life and getting all that God has for me—at an early age.

Lesson 4: Be an Eagle, Not a Chicken

Be real with yourself. Take a close look at your friends. Examine what you do when you are together. Examine what you talk about. Examine where you go. How do they influence the way you think, act, speak, and dress? More importantly, do they have a positive impact on your life? Do they share your love for God, your desire to live for Him? Are they people that can walk with you as you obtain His promises or will they keep you from those promises? You may find that there will be some friends that you have to cut off. But, don't be afraid or feel lonely. Think about the eagle. Yes, most times you spot an eagle by itself. But, that's because it is often on a mission either for food for its family, locating a safe place, or returning home again. It gains attention wherever it goes. People are drawn to watching it fly because of its great height and wings. This is how it will be with you. If you are willing to separate yourself in order to fulfill your purpose and obtain your inheritance, people will take notice of you. People will even be drawn to you because of your difference, your integrity, and your honesty. Remember God's promises. God will never ask you to give up something for nothing. He will bless you with all good things, including good friends.

One Final Lesson on Eagles

The bald eagle is the symbol for the United States of America. It is a symbol of justice, strength, and fairness, all of which are principles this country stands upon. One significant trait about bald eagles is that they are expert fliers. In order to fly as well as they do, they must remain strong and lightweight. They also have excellent vision, but only in the daytime. They experience difficulty seeing in the dark and, therefore, do most of their flying when there is plenty of light.

To remain an "eagle", you, too, must learn the art of being a good flier. Remain strong in your faith. Most importantly, let go of the baggage. The Bible encourages us in Hebrews 12:1 to *"Lay aside every weight that so easily besets us"*. Another version reads, *"Let us throw off everything that hinders and the sin that so easily entangles."* In order to fly high and obtain all that God has for you, you must let go of everything and everyone that is holding you back. Know that everyone cannot go where you are going, including your friends.

Secondly, dwelling in darkness will blind your vision. You are in darkness when you are not walking in God's Word. Psalms 119:105 says, *"Thy word is a lamp unto my feet, and a light unto my path."* It is God's Word that gives you direction, lighting your pathway to show you which way to go. His Word enlightens you and helps you to make wise decisions. Without the light of the Word, you cannot know which way to go. You cannot foresee harmful situations nor discern the true motives of

Lesson 4: Be an Eagle, Not a Chicken

those around you. This leads you into making mistakes and "flying" below your potential.

Practical Ways To Be, And Remain, An Eagle

1. Be a "history buff". Begin reacquainting yourself with the heroes of the Bible. There are great female heroines who walked in God's promises—Rahab, Ruth, Esther, Mary, the woman with the issue of blood, and many others. Draw strength from these women and try to walk in their examples. You can also draw from the strength of "modern day heroes". Look to the godly women around you and watch their walk with God. They are living examples.

2. Align yourself with people of like faith and mind. Remember, all people are not suitable for your design and purpose. They may be fun. They may be popular. They may even be fine. (Smile) But, are they good for you? Do they bring out the best in you? Be honest with yourself about whom you hang around and make the necessary adjustments. I am not saying not to talk to them or to be mean to them. You may not be able to go out with certain people or spend time with them outside of school. It may take you having a serious talk with your friends, letting them know that you are no longer going to do certain things or go

certain places. You may have to readjust your close circle of friends. Whatever the adjustments, make them, and stick to them.

3. Guard your ear gates and eye gates. Believe me. What you allow yourself to listen to, read, and watch will have an effect on you. If you hear and see certain things enough, you will begin to think on those things. Your imagination will take over. Eventually, you will act out those things or speak those things that you have seen and heard. They become a part of you. You need to make sure that you are cautious about the kind of material that you are taking in. Ask yourself, "Is this conversation, music, book, magazine, or movie building me up or drawing me closer to God?" If not, stay away from it!

4. Remind yourself of God's promises. Your mind needs to be renewed daily so that it can battle against the assaults and temptations that you will face. Repetition of these promises will ensure that they are imprinted in your mind, heart, and spirit. You can only lay hold to the promises if you know them and believe them.

Lesson Five:

"Run, Lady, Run!"

Scripture Reference: Genesis 39

Forrest Gump is one of my favorite movies. I love the simple innocence and uninhibited trust and love of the main character. Forrest is such a great character because he experiences so many of the situations that many of us go through—young, unrequited love, lost love, death, and merciless teasing for being different from everyone else. One of the things that helps Forrest through all of these experiences is his gift of running. Forrest runs from the bullies in his neighborhood. He runs from enemy fire. He also runs for a whole year when Jenny leaves him after they declare their love for one another. His running keeps him safe, helps him to release his feelings of anger and pain, and helps him to move on in a healthy, positive way that inspires others.

In this day and age, running is viewed as a sign of weakness. No one wants to run or back down for

Lessons for Young Ladies in Waiting

fear of being viewed as a punk or inferior to everyone else. Listen, ladies, there are times when running is absolutely necessary. Running can keep you out of dangerous situations. It can keep you from going pass the point of no return. Running can save you—physically, spiritually, and emotionally.

When I look back and think about it, I realize that so many of my indiscretions could have been avoided if I had the courage and the good sense to run. Yes, courage <u>and</u> good sense. Sadly, I possessed neither. Instead, I cared too much about looking foolish or like a little girl. I wanted to appear more knowledgeable than I was. I also had grown weary of the innocent, church girl role. Boys avoided me like the plague because I dressed a certain way and acted a certain way. Well, I wanted to be noticed, to feel pretty. So, I allowed myself to be open to certain things, believing I could control it. See, sex does not "just happen" There are actually lots of steps leading up to that final act. It starts with looks across the room and quick smiles. Then, you start "talking" and eventually you are "going out". Conversations become less innocent as suggestions are made during late night talks on the telephone. Instead of hanging out with friends, the two of you find more and more excuses to be left alone. Kisses become more passionate and long. Curiosity sets in. Soon, hands start reaching and groping. Before you know it, you are having sex. Sound familiar?

Lesson 5: Run, Lady, Run!

Well, this is the story of many young females. It starts out innocent enough, but things gradually, sometimes quickly, advance beyond their control. They begin doing things they said that they would never do because they are too afraid to say no. Sometimes it is not fear that prevents them from saying no. Simply put, it is all of the feelings that come with the late night talks, the time alone, the kissing, and the touching. Let's be real. For some girls, it feels good. It feels good to be kissed, to be touched, and to be wanted. Some girls find it exciting. Others confuse what they are feeling with love. So they wonder, "Why should I run from something or someone that makes me feel this way?!" Because, Dear Ones, what God has for you is so much better than a temporary fix. When you settle for the latter, you miss out on the good things that God has for you. Run away from the temptation and run to the One who can give you everything.

A Lesson in Running

I love the story of Joseph, one of the great men in the Bible. Joseph's brothers sold him into slavery due to their jealousy. But, Joseph never lost faith. See, God had showed Joseph in a series of dreams that he would be a great ruler one day. Joseph held on to his promise from God and walked in His ways. As a result, God was with him, and made his way prosperous. In fact, Joseph's master made him the overseer of his house and all that he had. In the midst of all of this, his master's wife fell for Joseph and lusted after him. Every day, she propositioned him, asking him to have sex with her. One day, she came on stronger than usual, grabbing on to his clothes, demanding that he sleep with her. What was Joseph's response? He ran, leaving his outer garment behind. Upset at his rejection, the woman accused Joseph of trying to rape her. Joseph was immediately cast into prison. But, God was with him even in this. Joseph gained favor in prison and the keeper of the prison gave him oversight over all of the prisoners. While in prison, Joseph interpreted the dreams of prisoners. One of them was Pharaoh's chief butler, who informed Pharaoh of Joseph's ability. After Joseph interprets one of Pharaoh's dreams, Pharaoh makes him ruler over all the land of Egypt!

It may seem that Joseph's running caused him more harm than good, but there are several important aspects to his story. First, Joseph had a promise from God. God promised Joseph that he would be prosperous. He promised Joseph that he had a great destiny before him—to be a great ruler. Second, Joseph believed in this promise, and this belief caused him to act differently. Joseph did not carry himself like a slave. Instead, he carried himself with honor and integrity even before his position of honor was realized in the natural. Third, because Joseph walked with God and believed the promise, he refused to let anyone or anything keep

Lesson 5: Run, Lady, Run!

him from pleasing God and, thus, missing out on the promise. He ran away from his master's wife not because he was a punk or less of a man. Joseph ran because he knew what was at stake. He represented God, and any stain on his reputation was a reflection of God. Joseph wanted to represent his God well. Also, he did not want to miss out on his destiny.

Joseph's story is so meaningful and applicable when it comes to young people today because many of you do not know that you have a destiny. God has plans for you. God told Jeremiah that:

> *Before I formed thee in the belly, I knew thee; and before thou camest forth out of the womb I sanctified thee, and I ordained thee a prophet unto the nations."*
>
> Jeremiah 1: 5

Just like Jeremiah, God knew you and set a purpose for your life even before you were born on this earth. He sanctified you. In other words God said, *"You are mine, beloved! I took the time to form you, to know you. You are so special to me that I desire to separate you unto myself so that you can be used for my glory and receive everything good that I have just for you."* Do you believe this? If you do, then you will know why you need to run from even the appearance of evil and the slightest temptation. Too much is at stake! Your destiny is before you. Run to it!

You may think that you are not strong enough, but you are. The Bible says in First Corinthians 10:13 that:

There is no temptation taken you but such is common to man: but God is faithful, who will not suffer you to be tempted above that you are able; but will with the temptation also make a way to escape, that ye may be able to bear it.

See, there is always an escape route for God's people. We choose to ignore it and suffer the consequences later. One day, the consequences may be too great. Learn to take the escape route and run!

Practical Tips for Running

1. Go out in groups. This first tip is the easiest. If you never put yourself in the position to be alone with a guy, the temptation will not be as strong or may not even be present.

2. Go out in groups in <u>public.</u> Do not fall into the trap of getting together over someone's house. Nine times out of ten, someone's parents will not be home or someone's parents are not watchful and responsible. Thus, it leaves you in the situation of being vulnerable to peer pressure. If your peers "pair off" like they did when I was growing up, you may feel the need to go along with doing what everyone else is

Lesson 5: Run, Lady, Run!

doing. If you are already in a group where people are couples, just know that you have been set up, and the "outing" has been orchestrated for a purpose.

3. Make sure that you have friends who are saved, love the Lord, and are really trying to live for Him. This way, you have some people you can lean on—people who are your own age and people who will not steer you in the wrong direction.

4. Have an older accountability partner. Although having saved friends your age is great, their knowledge is limited. You need someone who has been walking with the Lord longer than you. It does not have to be someone in their forties or fifties. Choose someone you trust and are willing to talk to. This way, when certain feelings and temptations do arise, you can go to this wiser adult who will pray with you and take you to God's word. Set it up so that if you are ever in a situation you are not comfortable with, you can call this person, and he/she can come get you or talk you through it.

5. Don't enter into a dating relationship. I am sure that this will be a very unpopular tip; however, if you do not allow yourself to get serious about/with an individual, it is more difficult for temptations to overcome you or even arise. In today's world, it is acceptable for

children and teenagers to say that they have a boyfriend/girlfriend or that they are "going out with someone". Some people even think that it is cute and harmless at certain ages. Well, it is not! You should not put claims on anyone or allow anyone to put claims on you until God sends you your husband. Plus, everyone you know, male and/or female, is still trying to find themselves just like you are. Does it make sense to be in a serious relationship with someone who does not even know who he is yet?

6. Pray. Prayer will keep you out of many situations. Pray before you go out and ask God to guide you. Pray about your friends so that God can send you godly friends. If you happen to find yourself in a situation, pray. God will provide a way of escape.

Lesson 6:

Don't Believe The Hype

Scripture Reference: John 8:44

One of the devil's greatest desires is to get us to stray from God and, as a result, forfeit our blessings. He wants to cause us to look away from God and His Word because he knows if we hold onto God and His Word, we will walk into all of the good things God has for us. Satan knows that if he can cast an ounce of doubt in our mind concerning God's character and His promises, we will cause ourselves to miss out. The way He accomplishes this is through telling us lies. The devil does not tell bold, outright lies; he twists the truth. He dresses his lies up just enough to tempt us and get our eyes off of what we know to be true. He has been doing this from the beginning. Eve is the perfect example.

When God created Adam and Eve, He gave them dominion over Eden and everything that was in it. They had everything they needed and were living in splendor. God gave them one command to not eat from the tree of the knowledge of good and evil or they will surely die. In sneaks the devil. He goes to Eve and asks her about God's command. His question is an exaggeration of God's command, "Did God really say you must not eat from any tree in the garden?" Eve corrects him, but he has his opening. Satan tells Eve that she will not die, that God knew if they did eat of the tree that they would become like Him. Satan makes it seem as if God is putting limits on them, holding back the "good stuff". We all know the story. Eve eats from the forbidden tree and then convinces Adam to do the same. As a result of their disobedience, Adam and Eve experience "death", which is separation from God. They are banished out of Eden.

There are several important points to this story. First, notice how Satan deceived Eve. He put her focus on that which she was forbidden to eat, suggesting that God is keeping something good for her away from her. Eve forgets all about the splendor of Eden. She forgets that she has everything she needs without any effort on her part. Suddenly, Eve wants the one thing she should not have. Second, it was easy for Adam and Eve to sin because they took their eyes off of God. Eve failed to trust God's character and instead trusted in her own wisdom to do what she felt was right. Adam trusted in Eve. Third, once Adam and Eve did eat from the tree, their eyes became open. They

Lesson 6: Don't Believe the Hype

experienced shame because now they were aware of evil. Finally, as a result of their disobedience, Adam and Eve lost everything. Although it started with Satan's deception, it was their choices and actions that caused this. Satan accomplished his goal—to get them to forfeit their own blessing.

Nothing has changed. Satan is still using deception and lies to get God's people to cause themselves to miss out on the blessings that He has for them. In today's day and age, he uses whomever and whatever he can. This is especially true among young people. Let's face it. There has never been a time like now when your minds, hearts, eyes, and ears are being exposed to so much via books, radio, television, and the Internet. Then there are the things that are passed on by word of mouth to you from your peers. I believe that Satan has staged a strategic attack to distract and deceive you. He wants you to believe his lies about everything, especially sex.

It's Not Like It Seems

Sex is widely portrayed today. It is used as a selling tool in advertisements. It is a popular subject in books, magazines, and talk shows. It is on display in movies, television sitcoms, and even music videos. Today, there is an outbreak of television shows with young people in high school and/or college who engage in careless sex without consequences. They change partners from season to season. Then there are the images of beautiful people who seem perfectly matched and madly in love. They "make love" to soft music with candlelight in the background. They rarely argue and, when they do, they make up by having "hot, passionate" sex. All of these images feed people's minds with false perceptions about what sex is. The act that God intended to be sacred, private, and shared between a husband and his wife is now on regular, public display for all eyes to see. In addition, it is rare for sex to be portrayed between a loving, married couple. In fact, married couples are often seen as having very little sex. Sex between married couples is also seen as boring or a chore.

The devil loves that the media is putting these images in the minds of young people like you. He wants to distort God's purpose and design for sex, making you believe that sex outside of marriage is more fun, enjoyable, and without consequence. But, you must remember John 8:44:

> *He (the devil) was a murderer from the beginning, and abode not in the truth because there is no truth in him. He is a liar and the father of it.*

Thus, what he is showing you is not like it seems. That's why it is so important to know what God has to say about sex, so that when you do see the images on television and in magazines or get

Lesson 6: Don't Believe the Hype

images in your mind from what you hear from your peers, you can recognize them for what they really are—false realities used by the devil to deceive and tempt you. I will cover what God has to say about sex in the next chapter. Because I do not want you to be ignorant of the devil's tactics, here's a list of some of the lies that I fell for. Learn from my mistakes.

Lie #1: Sex means love. So many people equate sex with love, especially those of our gender. I fell for it myself. I believed the guy that I gave my virginity to loved me. I actually justified my having sex with him because we loved each other. I even thought we would date throughout high school and college, and then get married. I was living in a dream world! I felt connected to him because not only had I given him my virginity, but I had almost been the mother of his child. But, I was foolish. He did not love me; neither did the guys that followed him. In truth, I have to admit that I really did not love them either. How can I say that? True love is patient. It is kind and selfless. It also endures all things. If the guy truly loved me, he would have never consented to my giving him such a precious gift when he was not my husband. I continued having sex with other guys because I was selfish and needy, trying to fill the emptiness inside. There was no real love between me and any of those guys because real love would have been patient and endured through celibacy. Do not fall for a guy who says, "I want to make love to you" or tells you that sex is a way for you to show your love. Real love says, "I am not going to allow you to do with your body what God has said that you should not do."

Lie #2: It is okay to have sex before marriage if you're in love, and/or you know that you are going to get married. Not! Wrong is wrong. Sin is sin. There is no justification for sin. God's commands do not change to suit our desires and feelings. You are no different from anyone else; your relationship is no different from anyone else's relationship. God has no respect of persons. Please, do not tell yourself, "God understands. He knows how I feel. He knows how much we love each other." The only thing that God understands is that you are knowingly and boldly disobeying Him.

Lie #3: As long as there is no penetration, what I do with a guy is okay because I am still a virgin. So many girls fall into the trap of believing that they are "okay" because they have not experienced sexual intercourse. They actually are proud of the fact that they are still "in-tact", and are not like the other girls. Well, let me enlighten you. Pure virginity is being untouched and unblemished. It means that you do not allow anyone to invade your "sacred space". Your body does not belong to you, so it is not yours to give to anyone to use as a

Lesson 6: Don't Believe the Hype

plaything. Nor should you be using a guy as a plaything, putting your hands or your mouth on places where they do not belong. For those of you who are "just messing around", you really are playing a dangerous game. You may think that you are practicing self-control and are safe, but you are not. All you are doing is waking feelings and desires that are not supposed to surface until your wedding night. You are also not safe, because eventually, you will give in because "messing around" will not be enough.

Lie #4: My friends are the best people to talk to about sex. Nothing could be further from the truth. I am sure that you have a friend or friends who seem very knowledgeable about everything, including sex. Their so-called knowledge sometimes comes from claimed firsthand experience. They share their sex stories with you and/or the stories of others. They talk about what they have seen on television or read in books and magazines. Let's be real. Most of what they share is not reality. Some of them are not as experienced as they would like everyone to believe. The information they dish out is often not based on fact. The television shows they watch and the material they read are false realities portrayed by the media and authors to make their work more appealing. No one your age or around your age can know any more than you do about sex just because they may have experienced it. When you want to know what sex is really about from a Christian perspective, it is the wrong move to go to your friends, especially if they are not saved. They may try to convince you that sex before marriage is natural and okay, things that are contrary to God's Word. Instead, turn to your parents, or find a trusted, saved, woman you can confide in.

Lie #5: If having sex before marriage was so wrong, God would stop me. You must remember that God is a gentleman. He does not force us to do anything. He wants us to choose to obey Him because we love Him. He wants us to do right because it is right. God is not going to stop you from doing anything. He has, however, provided you with His Word to teach you. The Holy Spirit is also there to guide you and convict you when you are wrong. Finally, God has placed people in your life who you can talk to when you are feeling vulnerable. God has given you the tools that you need to help you to abstain. Use the tools!

Practical Tips To Prevent You From Believing The Hype

1. Do your own research. There are books that have been written by Christian authors that talk about teen sex and sexuality from God's perspective. There are also Christian videos on the topic of teen dating and sex. All of these can

Lesson 6: Don't Believe the Hype

be useful, informative tools. Do not get your ideas about sex from the world.

2. Open up. No question is too stupid. No thought or opinion is unworthy of being shared. It is natural to wonder about the changes going on in your body and emotions. You may even be curious about sex. It is okay. Don't be silent or withdrawn. The devil uses this so that he can whisper lies in your ear and use others to do the same. Believing these lies will lead you into falling to temptation. I have said it several times in this book, and I will say it again. Find someone that you can talk to about what is going on in your body and your mind.

3. Do not engage in conversations about physical desires, physical activities, or actual sex with your friends—female or male. Avoiding these conversations will keep you from getting wrong information and from being pressured to try things that you know are not right. It also keeps feelings of lust and curiosity from stirring up, which can increase temptation.

Lessons for Young Ladies in Waiting

Lesson 7:

Keep It Real

Scripture Reference: John 8:32

One of the things that I most regret in those years that I had fallen away from God is my lack of honesty and integrity. I was not being real with myself, others, or God. In some ways, I allowed myself to be deceived. I believed the lies that the devil told me about sex. I believed that sex was a way to express love. I also believed that it was okay because I "loved" the guys that I had sex with. On the other hand, there were lies that I told myself to make me feel better. I knew that having sex before marriage was wrong. I just could not face that I was openly and willingly sinning before God. I lied, and told myself that my having sex was okay because I was not promiscuous. I told myself that God understood how much I was hurting; that I needed to feel loved and wanted. I needed to fill the emptiness inside.

But, God did not understand. He did not understand how I could confess my love for Him and then disobey Him so willingly and repeatedly. He did not understand why I would turn to men to give me something that only He could—unconditional love and wholeness. He did not understand why I continued down this road despite my becoming an emotional wreck. I was clingy and needy at times; while at other times, I was moody and easily frustrated. I was ignoring the truth. I was not real with myself. Now, it is one thing to lie to others. It is another thing to continually lie to yourself. This shows a lack of love and respect for yourself. It also shows an inability and/or a lack of desire to protect yourself from further harm. I was hurting so much, but I wouldn't, or couldn't, do anything about it. It wasn't until I was willing to face the truth that I could begin to heal.

Be Free

Imagine your hands and feet being tied up and bound tightly. You are enclosed in a tight, dark space. No matter how much effort you exert, how much pressure you put on the ropes, they will not break. You cannot see and can barely move. Your one desire is that someone will find you and set you free. Just when you are about to lose all hope, someone does find you, loosens the ropes, and helps you get free. Imagine the joy you would feel, the sense of relief. Afterwards, you vow that you

Lesson 7: Keep It Real

will never allow yourself to be in that position again. You will do all that you can to be and stay free. Now, many of you reading my book are not physically bound today; nor, are you fighting to maintain your physical freedom. You probably never even think about this possibility. But, are you aware that every day, the devil seeks to make you bound in your mind, spirit, and emotions? He seeks to hold you back and chain you down. Some of you have allowed the devil to do just that. You have listened to the devil's lies about your identity, worth, and destiny in God. You have believed the devil when he has told you that you are ugly, that you are not good enough. You have believed the devil when he told you that it is fun to have a boyfriend, and it's okay to be a tease. You have fallen for the eye candy he has placed in front of you, the things he has passed off as being better for you than what God has for you. You find yourself doing things that you said that you would never do, sneaking to places you said you would never go, and saying things you thought you would never say. You have lost your zeal for God. In fact, you have gotten to the point where you are indifferent towards the things of God. Or, you feel so guilty, you don't feel that you are worthy of going to God. The devil has you right where he wants you—buying into his lies and wandering further away from God. The only thing that can beat the devil and his lies is fighting him with the truth.

The Bible says in John 8:32 that *"Ye shall know the truth, and the truth shall set you free."* It sounds simple, huh? All you and I have to do to be free from any form of bondage is to know and walk in the truth concerning that thing that has us bound. For example, if I am bound by worry and anxiety, I just need to walk in the truth that says that I am not to be anxious over anything, but I am to present my requests to God. When I do this, God will give me peace. (See Philippians 4:6&7) So, if you are bound by sexual sin and the thoughts/feelings that result from it, then you need to seek the truth concerning sexual sin so that you can be free! It first starts with making a decision that you want to be free and then making a conscious effort to seek the truth. If it is that simple, why do so many of us stay in bondage?

You know the famous line, "You can't handle the truth!"? Well, this is true in the case of sexual sin. We cannot or will not look truth in the face. There are several reasons for this. First, if we are being real with ourselves, many of us do not want to face the truth because we know that we would have to admit that we have no business doing what we are doing. We enjoy it too much to stop, so we ignore the voice in our heads. Second, we do not want to face the truth because then we would have to face ourselves. We fear that we may not like what we see in terms of our behavior, words, actions, and appearance. Finally, we do not want to face the truth because in facing the truth, not only do we see ourselves, but we are forced to realize

Lesson 7: Keep It Real

that adjustments need to be made. This can be a painful process because the only way to make real life-changing adjustments is to go to God. When you do go to God, you have to be humble, open, repentant, and ready for change.

The Truth About Sex Before Marriage

Facing the truth about sex before marriage can be difficult in this day and age. There are so many different messages about sex—most of which are lies from the enemy to bind us to sexual sin. But, for every lie that the devil tells about sex before marriage, God has the truth if we ask Him. This is what I finally had to do in order to be rid of the emotional, spiritual, and mental baggage that I had been carrying as a result of my walking in sexual sin. I had to stop running from the truth and face it. I had to face myself and all of the ugliness, anger, pain, and resentment inside. I had to face my God. It was painful, but so worth it once I experienced freedom. Here is what God showed me about sex before marriage.

Truth #1: Sex is more than just physical. Many people limit sex to just a physical act. There is a lot of emphasis on safe sex, protecting one's body from sexually transmitted diseases and unwanted pregnancies. Little to nothing is said, however, about protecting one's spirit and emotions. We are made in God's image, thus we are spiritual beings. When you have sex with someone, you are laying down with his spirit. It is just as the Bible says, "the two become one". You are making yourself one with another human being—body and spirit. Therefore, when you get up, you carry a piece of him with you—good and bad. Imagine if you have multiple partners before you get married how many traces of those individuals will be in you. How will their spirits affect you in your marriage? More importantly, how will the emotional and mental baggage from those broken relationships affect how you relate to and think about your husband? I know that I had to really pray for God to help me to stop equating sex with something that was nasty or dirty. Because I had sex outside of marriage, I did not see it for the beautiful act that it was. It was something I did out of my pain and anger. Once I got married, it was difficult initially for me to be free with my husband when we were intimate. I had to remember that the marriage bed was clean and holy before God and that I could enjoy sex with my husband without fear of repercussion. Before we got married, I also had to work on not comparing my husband to the other guys that I dated. He was and is not them. I had to purge myself from those past relationships so that I could walk into my marriage whole.

Truth#2: Having sex before marriage separates you from God. The Bible warns us to "*Flee fornication. Every sin that a man doeth is*

Lesson 7: Keep It Real

without the body; but he that committeth fornication sinneth against his own body." (First Corinthians 6:18) I discussed earlier in the book how your body is not your own; it belongs to God. Everything that we do with our body should glorify God. When we have sex before marriage (fornicate), it is the one sin that we are doing that is violating the sacredness of our bodies. Our bodies are meant to be set apart for God's use. Not our own. Thus, when we have sex before marriage, we separate ourselves from God in that we deny His right to our bodies. God cannot use us if we are unclean. We cannot fulfill our purpose on earth if God does not do it through us.

Truth#3: Your virginity is a gift that only your earthly husband is worthy of receiving. Yes, it is a gift. It is not something to be taken lightly and given to the first guy you think you love or to the first guy who shows you any kind of attention. It is a precious gift. Think about it. Would you spend your money and buy a nice gift from the store for just anybody? Most of you would say no. Well, if you value your money so much that you would not spend it on just anybody, is not your body more valuable than your money?! Your virginity is not only valuable; it is priceless. Nothing can replace it. Once it is gone, it is gone. See, something special happens when you lose your virginity. God gave each of us (females) a hymen, which slightly covers the vaginal opening. When penetrated, the hymen tears, and bleeding results. This blood mixes with the fluid of your partner during intercourse. God intended for you not to lose your virginity until marriage because what occurs during that first act represents a blood covenant between you and your husband. A blood covenant is the strongest type of covenant there is; it can never be broken or changed. This is how God intended it to be. He does not desire for you to have one partner after another, giving yourself away piece by piece. He does not desire for you to experience heartache from broken relationships. Instead, He wants you to wait on the one that He has just for you, and to be able to present yourself to him—unashamed and unblemished. He desires you to have one earthly husband who will cherish you and love you just as Christ loves the church.

Truth#4: Sex inside of marriage is natural, beautiful, and pleasurable. Some people will tell you that it is natural to experiment with physical activity and/or sex when you are young. Again, if it is outside of God's will for you, it is not natural! There are lies being fed to you by your peers and the media that will lead you to believe that sex when you are young and single is good, that you have to get it while you can. Some of you may have even been led to believe that once you get married, that sex is boring because you are with the same person for the rest of your life. This is not the case. God intended for sex inside of marriage to be beautiful and pleasurable

Lesson 7: Keep It Real

for both partners. Even the Bible talks about the pleasures of sex inside of marriage. For example, The Song of Solomon is all about King Solomon and his bride. In the book, they express a very passionate love for one another. Proverbs 5:18-20 admonishes men to *"rejoice with the wife of their youth"* and speaks of women being satisfying to their husbands. God created sex for marriage. It is His design. Everything that God designs is good when we do it His way!

Practical Tips For Keeping It Real

1.   Continue to seek after Him. Do not get lax in pursuing a close walk with Christ, which some of us do. We take it for granted that we are saved and, therefore, automatically going to heaven. We do not seek to do anything else and simply go through the motions. Your walk should be a priority. Knowing Him more should be your desire. Jesus declared in John 14:6 that He is *"the way, the truth, and the life."* Once you come to know Jesus and work on walking with Him every day, you will come to know the truth. The truth about all things lies in Him. Whatever questions you have, you can find the answers in Him. Whatever you are seeking, whatever you desire is in Him because He is the way and the life. There is so much more to being saved than going to church and singing in the choir! God is calling us to something deeper and more fulfilling.

2. Do reality checks periodically. You want to take a close look at yourself and your walk. Have you been walking in integrity? In what ways have you not been real with yourself, others, or with God? If there are any signs of falsehood, get it straight by asking God to help you make the necessary adjustments in your life so that you can be a young lady of integrity and honor.

3. Be real about your struggles. Everyone has issues. Everyone has truths that they need to face. First, go to God and confess what you are struggling with. Next, ask the Holy Spirit to guide you to someone who can counsel you and who will pray with you. You also want this person to be someone who will be real with you and not just pat you on your back. This person should be able and willing to tell you the truth even if it will hurt you. It should also be someone who has either been fully delivered from this struggle or who has not encountered this struggle. It makes no sense to go to someone who is struggling with the same thing. You may just end up enabling each other to continue to justify and indulge in your area of struggle.

4. Study, study, study! After you go to God and face the fact that you do have a struggle, you have to take action. I mentioned seeking someone out who can pray with and talk to you. You must also seek truth for yourself. You can turn to the

Lesson 7: Keep It Real

Word of God. You can also get tapes, devotionals, and books that discuss how to be free from sexual sin. You must be proactive in order to beat the devil at his own game. He uses books, C.D.'s, DVD's, magazines, etc. to fill your head with lies. You must use the same things to replace those lies with truth!

Lessons for Young Ladies in Waiting

Lesson 8:

It's a Love Thang

Scripture Reference: I John 4:19

One of the basic emotional needs of every human being is love. From the time of birth, we seek out the love of those closest to us. Studies have shown that babies who thrive and grow into emotionally and mentally healthy children, experienced positive, loving interactions with primary caregivers. Love is what we need to feel safe and secure, capable and worthy. The desire for love is so strong that when not given, it can drive people to look for it in negative, unproductive ways. These people can become misguided and desperate in their pursuit of love. Once they find love, they often do not know how to simply receive it and enjoy it. They either manipulate to keep that love, or they become needy and latch on as tight as they can, driving that love away.

There may be some of you reading my book right now who are also searching for love. You want to feel loved, to feel wanted. You may have the love of both parents, but for some reason, you still long for more. You want a relationship, to know the love of someone other than your family and friends to validate your desirability and worthiness. Or, you may be missing the love of a mother or a father. You desire someone to fill that void that is missing from your life. You may have suffered abuse—verbal, physical, sexual, or emotional. As a result, you do not even know how to define love. You may have lost faith in its existence. You may feel that you are undeserving of love. You have given your love away cheaply. You have sold yourself short, unaware of your true value. You have been needy or you have been manipulative in your attempt to hold on to love. But, if you are real with yourself, you will admit that it has not been working. You are still left feeling unfulfilled. Some of you may even feel ashamed, guilty, and dirty. You may feel foolish and used at times.

Whatever your reason for searching and whatever the results have been, I declare that your search can be over! You do not have to make mistake after mistake after mistake. You do not have to enter into ungodly relationships in search of something—be it love, good feelings, or just a good time. You do not have to search because the love that you need is already available to you!

There Is No Greater Love

The Bible says that God is love. Love is the very essence of who He is. Everything that God does is

Lesson 8: It's A Love Thang

born out of His love for us. He has proven His love for us time and time again. First, He did it when He created this world. Who did He put at the center of the universe—mankind? He had us on His mind before we were even born! Ephesians 1:4 lets us know that He chose us <u>before</u> the foundation of the world. Jeremiah 1:5 tells us that before we were even conceived in the womb, God knew us and already sanctified us (set us apart) to be used by Him. God saw us as worthy from the beginning. Not only did He see us as worthy. He blessed us. The first thing God did after creating mankind was bless it. God showed His love for us by creating us, making us the center of the universe by giving us dominion over all of the earth. He blessed us from the beginning, empowering us to do the work He had sanctified us to do.

Second, God showed His love by sending His only son. He was willing to watch His son suffer and die a horrible death so that we would turn back to Him. In doing this, God showed that He was willing to give His very best to show His love. He also showed how important having a close relationship with all of us is to Him. God could have just destroyed the world at that moment. He could have sent legions of angels to rescue Jesus, but no. Jesus' act on the cross made it possible for all of us to know God's love forever. He knew that there were more of His children yet to be born, more of His children yet to come into right relationship with Him. He knew that you would be one of them.

Finally, God continues to show His love in that He pursues us and draws us to Him. His love keeps going. Jeremiah 31:3 says, *"I have loved thee with an everlasting love: therefore with loving kindness have I drawn thee."* That's what I love about God. There is nothing that you or I can do or not do to make God stop loving us. Earthly relationships may require you to do certain things or meet certain requirements before you receive love. God is not like that. He gives and shows His love for us no matter what. He keeps looking out for us, protecting us, and keeping us. Even when we turn away from Him, He is still there. In addition, God shows His love by not being forceful or manipulative. He is who He says He is. He comes with no tricks or hidden agendas. He does not make us love Him. Instead, God is gentle and kind. He is open and pure, patiently waiting for us to fall in love with Him simply because of who He is. God wants us to get to the point where we know that His love is and always will be greater than any love we will ever know. Why? Because He loved us first. He loved us before we were even thought of, before our parents laid eyes on us. He loved us before we even thought of doing anything for Him. God loved us before we loved Him. His love is steadfast and will remain forever.

Don't Fall For A Lesser Love

The Bible is filled with love stories. I mean, these are stories that could make great soap operas and even movies. One of the most interesting is the story of

Lesson 8: It's A Love Thang

Hosea and Gomer. Now, Gomer was a known prostitute. After they got married Gomer continued to prostitute herself. In addition, she had two children as a result of her affairs. Despite this, Hosea goes and retrieves his wife. He actually had to pay money to buy her back before he could take her home! Now, the twist to this story is that God commanded Hosea to marry this woman. God knew she was a whore. He knew she would cause Hosea heartache with her continued cheating. But, He also knew that she would eventually be won over by Hosea's consistent, unfailing love and devotion.

God uses Hosea's marriage as an illustration of Israel's continued faithlessness to Him. Hosea's reconciliation with his wife and the restoration of their marriage is what God desired for His chosen people. If you are familiar with the Old Testament, than you know about God's constant pursuit of His chosen people, the Israelites. From the time that He brought them out of Egypt, God was showering love on them.

They never worried about what they would eat or drink. Their clothes or shoes never wore out in all of the years they were traveling to get to the Promise Land. They were protected from their enemies. In short, they were lacking nothing. You would think that the Israelites would be content. However, they were not, Instead, they grumbled and complained at the slightest inconvenience. They even thought and spoke about turning back and returning to Egypt and a life of slavery! Because of their lack of love for and trust in God, a whole generation of Israelites was not allowed to enter the Promise Land. Even after entering the Promise Land, the Israelites allowed themselves to be tempted to stray from God. They turned their love and devotion to lesser gods. The Israelites served these gods. They even did speechless things to earn the favor of these gods, such as offering their children as burnt sacrifices and committing immoral sexual acts. In all this, God was still willing to take them back. God said in Hosea 3:19-20:

And I will betroth thee unto Me forever; yea, I will betroth thee unto Me in righteousness, and in judgment, and in loving kindness, and in mercies. I will even betroth thee unto Me in faithfulness: and thou shalt know the Lord.

In other words, God was in it to win it. He determined that they would be His forever. God made a covenant long before He brought the Israelites out of Egypt with their forefathers. He promised that He would be their God, that He would love them, and that He would make them great. God was bound by that covenant, by the words that came out of His mouth. He would see to it that the covenant came to pass despite the Israelites continued unfaithfulness.

God's love is given freely. The only thing that He asks in return is something that all of us ask of those we love on earth—to show love in return. He also asks for our loyalty. Too many times, however, we act like the Israelites. For some reason God's love is not enough. We look to lesser gods. You may say,

Lesson 8: It's A Love Thang

"Wait a minute. I'm not sacrificing animals or going to temples praying to some unknown god." I am not talking about that. A lesser god is anyone or anything that we make a priority over our relationship with God. It is anyone or anything that takes our focus off of Him and His desire for our lives. This person or thing causes us to do things and say things that are contrary to God's Word. So, who or what is your lesser god? Is it a relationship with a boy that you know you should give up, but refuse? Is it an activity or hobby? Is it a movie or rap star? Could it be television or the Internet? Could it be your friends? Anyone or anything that takes precedence over your walk with God, that causes you to lose your desire for Him, is a lesser god in your life.

Like I said before, God is a gentleman. He will never force Himself on you. Nor is it His desire to make you love Him with all of yourself. However, our turning from Him and offering what is rightfully His to someone or something else is not without consequence. When the Israelites refused to return to God, He allowed them to suffer the natural consequences of serving lesser gods. These gods could not protect them and save them in their time of trouble, and trouble did come frequently. When trouble came, God was willing to deliver them out of that trouble. The Israelites turned back to God for a little while, but then returned to their old ways. Eventually, God let them go their own way. Romans 1: 26-32 speaks of how God *"gave them up into vile affections…God gave them over to a reprobate mind, to do those things which are not convenient."* This is when the people began indulging in all kinds of sin adultery, homosexuality, fornication, murder, being disobedient to parents, gossiping, backbiting, coveting, etc. This is all because they no longer recognized and cherished the love of God or the significance of loving Him in return.

Even today, God will pursue us and continue to draw us with His love. But, there will come a point when He will release us to do our own thing. In my case, I knew God. I went to church. I had heard that sex before marriage was wrong, but I continued to indulge in and justify my sin. My boyfriend became a lesser god in my life. Fulfilling his needs and making him happy became more important than doing what God said. As a result, I had to suffer consequences for my sin. I must admit, that for a long time, I believed that God made my miscarriage happen. I soon had to realize that my having unprotected sex led to my getting pregnant, which unfortunately led to a miscarriage. A miscarriage is something that can occur to any woman. I happen to be one of them. It was not something God did to me. God is not like that. He did not need to give me a miscarriage so that I would turn to Him. Instead, He continued to draw me with His love. In fact, He sent me help when the devil was trying to get me to take my own life. God let me live! He waited patiently until I came to my right mind and turned back to Him.

Lesson 8: It's A Love Thang

His Love (And Grace) Is Sufficient

It is hard to fathom the love of God. No other love compares to His love. His love is so big! It is so big that it can reach across the world. It is so big that it can cover and forgive every sin. It is so big that it can heal the deepest hurt. I do not know where you are in your walk with God. I do not know if you have fully realized the depth of His love for you. But, it is God's desire that we not only know His love, but that we are filled with the fullness of all He is. (Eph. 3:19) There is no ending to His love. His love is more than enough. It is all sufficient. This means it satisfies, and is adequate to the individual's wants. In other words, whatever you need or want, God's love is what you need to satisfy that need or want!

Not only is His love sufficient, but so is His grace. Grace refers to both the love and favor of God being freely extended to you. It is also the divine influence or empowering that renews your heart and helps restrain you from a life of sin. Some of you may be thinking that you do not have what it takes to love God the way He deserves to be loved. The devil may have you believing that you do not have what it takes to live your life as a saved young person. He may have you thinking it's too hard, so you just need to stay on the road you are on. After all, the road the devil is offering looks more fun and carefree. Let me tell you, in the end, the devil will try to destroy and kill you just like he did me. If you desire to live for God, to know His love, and to love Him with your entire being, His love will satisfy and meet that desire. His grace will empower you to live for Him. All you have to do is turn to and completely surrender to Him.

Practical Ways to Know God's Love

1. Inspect your life for signs of lesser gods. Is there anyone or anything that is getting in the way of your walk with God? Is there anyone or anything keeping you from reading your Word, praying, or going to church regularly? Have you put the happiness and needs of someone else before God's will for your life? Have you begun to do things that go against what you know to be right? If you find any lesser gods, get rid of them. Cold turkey is the best way. Do not try to ease out of that friendship or relationship slowly. Do not "wean" yourself off of that television show or Internet. Remember, God will give you the grace you need.

2. Repent of any ongoing sin that you have allowed yourself to indulge in. If there is a sin that you are struggling with, it is hindering you from fully knowing God's love. Why? Because God cannot dwell where sin abides. Even though He is still with you and He still loves you, it will be difficult for you to experience and feel His love. Think about it. When you disappoint your parents, isn't it hard for you to be around them or look at them? Well, we are the same way when it comes to God. When we continue to knowingly sin, it is

Lesson 8: It's A Love Thang

hard to be in His presence. It is hard to read His Word and pray. We experience guilt, which makes it hard to feel His love.

3. Hang around people who reflect God's love. God often expresses His love for you through others. How will you recognize God's love in others? Read First Corinthians 13, which tells you what love truly is. This way, you will not fall for the counterfeiters.

Lessons for Young Ladies in Waiting

Lesson 9:

True Love Waits

Scripture Reference: Deuteronomy 6:5; Isaiah 40:31

"God please take this desire away from us. Please help us to keep it dormant until we are married." David prayed through tears streaming down his face. At that time it was early in our relationship, but David and I knew that God had called us together. We knew that one day we would be married. However, neither David nor I were virgins. We had both made the mistake of having sex before marriage. This was both of our first attempts at having a pure relationship. It was difficult, and we fell. Actually, we fell three times. But, something happened after that third time. The Holy Spirit convicted us. We were so burdened afterwards that we both began to cry. David led us in prayer, and together we made the commitment to never have sex before marriage again. We kept that commitment to God. It was hard work. But, the one thing that kept us was our love. We loved each other enough to wait. We loved each other enough to not allow one another to sin against God. More importantly, we loved God. Our love for God far outweighed our physical desires. Because we put our love for God first, God's love and grace empowered us to do what was right. Not only that, but God also gave me what I earnestly desired on our wedding night—to feel like it was my first time all over again. It was the most beautiful night of my life.

Abstaining from sex before marriage is not something you can do on your own. You cannot just make a decision and think that you are going to stick by it. Your flesh is weak, and it will have certain desires. The thing that will keep you is love. No, I am not speaking of God's love. God will love you regardless. I am speaking of your love for God. David and I loved each other a lot. We still do. But, it was our love for God that kept us. We loved Him so much that we did not want to disappoint Him. We loved Him so much that we wanted to be pleasing to Him. We loved Him so much that we did not want to be separated from Him as a result of sin.

Lesson 9: True Love Waits

The Greatest Command

God commands in Deuteronomy 6:5

And thou shalt love the Lord thy God with all thine heart, and with all thy soul, and with all thy might.

In Deuteronomy 8:18, God commands, *"But thou shalt remember the Lord thy God..."* Then, a few chapters over in Deuteronomy 10:12, He says,

And now, Israel, what doth the Lord thy God require of thee, but to fear the Lord thy God, to walk in all His ways, and to love Him, and to serve the Lord thy God with all thy heart and with all thy soul.

What does all of this mean? When you love God with all of your heart and soul, it means that you have surrendered your emotions, your thoughts, and will to God. When you love Him with all of your might, you are saying, "God, I am putting all of my strength and energy into loving you!" Remembering God means just that—not letting a day go by that you do not acknowledge Him and the fact that you need Him. Fearing God is not about being afraid of or frightened by God. It is about having a high regard and respect towards God. Finally, walking in His ways refers to following God's commands. Do not believe the lie that God understands that you are young, that this is your time to have fun, experiment, and, do your own thing until you are "ready" to surrender all to Him. The devil is a liar! God can grace you in your teens and your twenties to live for Him.

If you are familiar with the Old Testament, you know that the theme of loving God with all of yourself is repeated throughout. In the New Testament, Jesus Christ reminds us again, referring to loving God as the most important command. What strikes me is that God felt the need to remind us repeatedly in His Word to love Him, to not forget Him, and to serve Him. Why? After all, He is the one who loves us unconditionally. Yet, we need to be reminded to love, remember, fear, and serve Him. God knew that we would allow ourselves to lose focus. We would allow ourselves to get distracted and pulled away by what the devil dangles in our face. He cared about us enough that He put those reminders in His word, so that we would know to turn back to Him.

What's Love Got To Do With It?

If you are struggling with any sin, including sexual sin, then your love for God is the key. If you have any need or desire for your life, then your love for God is the key. If you are lacking self-esteem, self-respect, and self-love, then your love for God is the key. If you are having problems with waiting for any type of physical intimacy until you are

Lesson 9: True Love Waits

married, then your love for God is the key. Let me show you.

1. From the scriptures above, we know that God can see our love for Him when we follow after His ways. I already advised you of repenting of any sin that you are continuing to indulge in, but how do you keep from falling into that sin again? If you love God with all of your heart, soul, and might, then you will focus your emotions and thoughts towards God. Your strength and energy will be focused on loving God. So, instead of getting your emotions tied up in an ungodly relationship, your heart will be wrapped up in God. Instead of thinking lustful thoughts, your thoughts will be on God and His goodness. Instead of using your strength and energy on activities that are ungodly, you will engage yourself in activities that will demonstrate your love for God.

2. I Peter 4: 8 tells us *"love covers a multitude of sin"*. When you turn back to God after repenting of your sin and focus your love on Him, you will experience the fullness of His love. With His love comes forgiveness and mercy. Your sin is no longer an issue between you and God. Thus, you can come into His presence without doubt, fear, shame, or guilt. This will free you to love Him even more.

3. Loving God leads to prosperity. (Psalm 122:6) Prosperity does not just refer to money and material gain. Prosperity refers to having fullness in every area of your life. There is nothing missing or lacking. You will have what you need physically, emotionally, mentally, and spiritually when you love God with all of your heart, soul, and might. This means low self-esteem, low self-respect, and lack of self-love have to go because you are whole emotionally. Negative and even impure thoughts and desires have to go because you are whole mentally. All that you need will come to you if you focus your love on God!

4. First Corinthians 13 gives us all of the characteristics of love. Love is patient, it does not behave itself unseemly, nor is it selfish. When you love God with all of your heart, soul, and might, you will learn how to wait patiently for all that He has for you. One of the things that God has for you is pure sexual relations with your husband. This is a promise from God. Not only will you wait patiently, but you will also not behave unlady like to obtain the promise before it is time. Finally, if you do date and actually believe that you love someone, you will not be so selfish as to take his body—something that does not belong to you, but to God.

Lesson 9: True Love Waits

What To Do While Waiting

You may be thinking, "Okay. This is easier said then done. There are some years in between my waiting and my receiving the promise. What do I do in the meantime?" You wait and wait. I know it sounds repetitive, but let me explain what I mean. There are two types of waiting that I am referring to. The first is to stay or rest in expectation or patience. First Corinthians 13 also says that love believes and hopes for all things. You have to believe that God has something better for you than broken hearts and broken relationships. He wants you to have more than sex. He wants you to be in covenant with a man who will cherish, honor, protect, and love you. Waiting does not mean you just sit. It also means actively praying for, confessing, and believing God for that future mate when He knows that you are ready for him. It also means making sure that you are a woman of prayer, faith, integrity, and honor that your future husband will be proud to claim as his own. While waiting you are in a position of rest. This means you are not desperately seeking. You do not get upset, frustrated, or depressed because you "don't have a man". Although you are praying and believing God for your future mate, that is not your focus or purpose. This leads me to the second type of waiting.

The second type of waiting is defined as performing the duties of a servant or attendant.

While waiting, you should be focusing on serving God. God has placed gifts and abilities in you that you can use to serve Him. He has placed something special in you that He needs to build His kingdom. He can use you to witness to other young ladies. He can use you as an example to the young and old. God can open doors for you to fulfill your greatest dreams if you are willing to serve Him.

While you are waiting—sitting patiently in great expectation while serving Him—God has another promise for you. Isaiah 40:31 promises *"But they that wait upon the Lord shall renew their strength; they shall mount up with wings as eagles; they shall run and not be weary; and they shall walk and not faint."* Wow! This scripture says it all. When you wait, God promises that He will give you strength. Whenever you are feeling weak and tempted, God will give you the strength that you need to overcome that temptation. Whenever you are tired, frustrated, and overwhelmed in life, God says that He will not allow you to faint or get weary. He will lift you up. Remember the chapter on being an eagle? Well, God promises that when you wait, He will give you the ability of eagles—to fly high above every circumstance and obstacle and obtain all that He has for you. See, there is a blessing in waiting and waiting!

Practical Ways to Love and Wait
1. Check your love life. God has called us to an intimate love relationship with Him. I have

Lesson 9: True Love Waits

already said that being saved is more than just going to church. God wants us to commune with Him, to know Him. He gave us His best, and continues to give us His all. Are you doing the same? If not, what part of yourself are you holding back from Him and why? When you identify those areas, ask God to help you to release them into His hands.

2. Make worship a lifestyle. Worship is recognizing God for who He is. You cannot fully love someone that you do not know. Who He is to you may not be who He is to someone else. For instance, he has revealed Himself to me as a lifesaver and a mind regulator because the devil was putting thoughts of depression and suicide into my mind, but God stepped in. Think about how God has revealed Himself to you. Write down all the things that God is to you and call those things out to Him daily. Worship will draw you into a more intimate love relationship with Him.

3. Find ways in which you can use your gifts and abilities to serve God. Most likely, God has already placed a desire in you to do something—sing, tutor, volunteer somewhere, dance, etc. Everyone has something that they can do for God. Whatever it is, do it unto Him.

My Prayer For You

I do not see this as the end of my book, but as a new beginning for you. I decided to write this book hoping and expecting by faith that it will reap a harvest of young ladies everywhere committing themselves to waiting. They will commit to waiting to have sex until marriage. They will also commit to patiently waiting and expecting all of the promises of God while serving Him. That is what a true lady in waiting is. She trusts that God knows what is best for her and keeps on believing. She knows who she is in Him and knows that she is worthy of and entitled to all God's promises. She commits to loving and serving Him in the midst of her waiting. This is my hope and expectation. It has been my prayer throughout my journey of writing this book. I continue to pray for you. I pray...

That you will come to know who you are in Him—royalty.

That you will carry yourself as the queen He has called you to be, that you will be ladylike, and that you will be a young lady of integrity and honor.

That you will believe and expect every promise that you are entitled to as an heir and patiently wait on those promises.

Lesson 9: True Love Waits

That you will not suffer from low self-esteem, low self-respect, or lack of self-love, but you will know that you are beautifully and wonderfully made.

That you will not seek for your worth in any relationship outside of your relationship with God.

That if you have fallen into sexual experimentation or having sexual intercourse that you make the decision to repent and abstain until you are married. Do not feel like it is too late and just wallow in your sin. No matter how much it may seem "natural" or "good", or how much the devil makes you think God will not forgive you, remember that he is a liar! Do not make the mistake that I did and spend time feeling like you are not worthy of God's love or forgiveness. God is waiting with open arms, ready to forgive you. All you have to do is make the first step, forgive yourself, and begin to heal.

That you will fully know God's love and fall in love with Him. There is truly no greater love!

Like I said at the beginning, I have not arrived. I made a lot of mistakes along the way. There are still times when I look back with regret, wishing I had done things differently. Those times are gradually decreasing. Thank God for His steadfast patience, grace, and love! Yes, I am a work in process, but I do continue to be a lady in waiting. I

Lessons for Young Ladies in Waiting

have a great expectation for what God is going to do in and through me. I hope that God is pleased with my service to Him in writing this book. Mostly, I hope that you will carry these lessons with you and that your love relationship with God will be full and complete. May you forever be blessed!

Special Note

Minister Anita is available for speaking engagements at church services, retreats, and seminars. She is also more than willing to share her story with young ladies in churches, youth groups, schools, and on college campuses.

For contact information, you can e-mail her at youngladiesinwaiting@hotmail.com.

Lessons for Young Ladies in Waiting

www.ingramcontent.com/pod-product-compliance
Lightning Source LLC
Chambersburg PA
CBHW060843050426
42453CB00008B/809